Big
Science Ideas

What are Earth's Biomes?

Bobbie Kalman

Crabtree Publishing Company

www.crabtreebooks.com

Big Science Ideas

Created by Bobbie Kalman

Dedicated by Peter and Bobbie
In loving memory of Alan Crabtree

Author and Editor-in-Chief
Bobbie Kalman

Editor
Kathy Middleton

Proofreader
Crystal Sikkens

Design
Bobbie Kalman
Katherine Berti
Samantha Crabtree (cover)

Production coordinator
Katherine Berti

Illustrations
Barbara Bedell: pages 1, 8, 9, 13, 22, 24 (starfish and clam)
Katherine Berti: pages 4, 7 (tree), 16, 24 (limpet)
Vanessa Parson-Robbs: page 24 (sea urchin)
Bonna Rouse: pages 24 (crayfish), 26 (sea turtle)
Margaret Amy Salter: pages 7 (all except tree),
    26 (octopus and sea slug)
Tiffany Wybouw: page 5

Photographs
© Dreamstime.com: page 30 (bottom left)
© Shutterstock.com: cover, pages 1, 3, 5, 6, 7, 8, 9,
    10 (except inset), 11, 12, 13, 15 (top left), 16, 17,
    18, 19, 20, 21 (except bottom left), 22, 23, 24, 25,
    26, 27, 28, 29, 30 (except bottom left), 31
Other images by Corel, Eyewire, and Photodisc

Library and Archives Canada Cataloguing in Publication

Kalman, Bobbie, 1947-
    What are earth's biomes? / Bobbie Kalman.

(Big science ideas)
Includes index.
ISBN 978-0-7787-3284-6 (bound).--ISBN 978-0-7787-3304-1 (pbk.)

    1. Biotic communities--Juvenile literature. I. Title. II. Series: Kalman,
Bobbie, 1947- . Big science ideas.

QH541.14.K3427 2009   j577   C2009-901257-X

Library of Congress Cataloging-in-Publication Data

Kalman, Bobbie.
    What are earth's biomes? / Bobbie Kalman.
        p. cm. -- (Big science ideas)
    Includes index.
    ISBN 978-0-7787-3304-1 (pbk. : alk. paper) -- ISBN 978-0-7787-3284-6
(reinforced library binding : alk. paper)
    1. Biotic communities--Juvenile literature. I. Title. II. Series.

QH541.14.K34968 2009
577--dc22

                                        2009008010

Crabtree Publishing Company

www.crabtreebooks.com   1-800-387-7650

Published in Canada
Crabtree Publishing
616 Welland Ave.
St. Catharines, Ontario
L2M 5V6

Published in the United States
Crabtree Publishing
PMB16A
350 Fifth Ave., Suite 3308
New York, NY 10118

Published in the United Kingdom
Crabtree Publishing
White Cross Mills
High Town, Lancaster
LA1 4XS

Published in Australia
Crabtree Publishing
386 Mt. Alexander Rd.
Ascot Vale (Melbourne)
VIC 3032

Contents

What are biomes?

A **biome** is a kind of natural environment, where certain plants grow. A biome also includes the animals that live in that environment. The plants and animals in a biome have **adapted**, or changed to suit, that biome.

What is climate?

Biomes have different amounts of sunlight and water. They also have different **climates**. Climate is the usual weather in an area. It includes wind, temperature, and **precipitation**, such as rain or snow. The climate of a biome has a lot to do with its location. Biomes are located in different areas and at different heights, such as high on mountaintops.

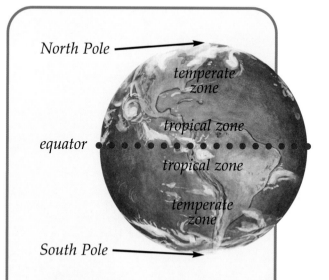

North Pole
temperate zone
tropical zone
equator
tropical zone
temperate zone
South Pole

What is the location?

Biomes near the North Pole or South Pole have long, dark, cold winters. **Tropical** biomes are warm all year because they are close to the **equator**, where it is always hot. **Temperate** biomes lie between the poles and the equator. They have both warm and cold weather and four seasons—winter, spring, summer, and autumn.

What are habitats?

Habitats are the natural homes of plants and animals.
There are many habitats in each biome. This pond is
a habitat that is part of the **freshwater biome**. Many
kinds of water plants grow in and around this pond
habitat. Frogs and fish live in or near the water.
Birds and insects visit it to find food to eat.

*Ocean water is called **salt water** because it contains a lot of salt.*
This pond is a freshwater pond. Fresh water does not contain a lot of salt.

Living and non-living

Earth's biomes are made up of **living things** and **non-living things**. Plants are living things. Animals are living things. Living things move, grow, change, and die. They also make new living things, such as new plants or baby animals.

Non-living things

Air, water, sunlight, soil, and rocks are examples of non-living things. Living things could not stay alive without non-living things.

Name two living things and three non-living things in this picture.

6

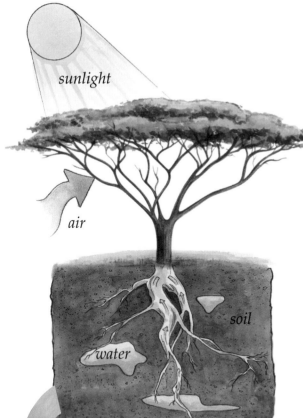

sunlight

air

soil

water

An acacia tree uses sunlight, air, and water to make food. It grows in soil.

What is an ecosystem?

An **ecosystem** is the way living things work together with the non-living things in a habitat. For example, plants use the **energy** in sunlight to make food from air and water. Unlike plants, animals cannot make food. To get energy, they must eat plants or other animals that have eaten plants. When an animal eats another animal that has eaten a plant, a **food chain** forms. An acacia tree, a giraffe, and a lion make up the food chain shown on this page.

This giraffe is getting the sun's energy by eating acacia leaves.

A lion is eating the giraffe. The sun's energy is being passed along from the acacia, to the giraffe, to the lion.

Earth's biomes

The same kinds of biomes can be found in many places on Earth. For example, forests are almost everywhere, and there are different kinds of forests. In the pictures on these pages, you can see six main biomes: **forest**, **desert**, **grassland**, **tundra**, **marine**, and fresh water. Each of these biomes has different kinds of habitats and ecosystems.

The main plants in a forest biome are trees. The forest biome also has other plants and many kinds of animals. Learn about forests on pages 10-13.

Deserts are dry biomes. Some deserts are very hot and sandy. Other deserts are not as dry or hot. See deserts on pages 18-21.

Grasslands are dry, windy, grassy areas. Some grasslands have bushes and many trees, as well. See pages 14-17 to learn about grasslands.

Tundra biomes are dry areas without any trees. They are found on high mountains and near the North Pole. (See pages 22-23.)

Oceans make up the marine biome. Parts of oceans are sunny and warm. Parts are dark and cold. See pages 24-27 to learn about oceans.

This alligator lives in a river. Rivers, lakes, ponds, and **wetlands** are parts of the freshwater biome (see pages 28-29).

Boreal forests

Forests are very important because trees give us clean air. They use up harmful **carbon dioxide** and make **oxygen**, the gas in air that we need to breathe. There are different kinds of forests. **Boreal** forests, also known as **taiga**, are in the northern areas of the world and near the tops of mountains. Boreal forests have long, dry winters and short summers. The main type of trees that grow in these forests are **conifers**. Conifers are evergreen trees with cones.

Wolves, owls, hawks, and lynxes hunt in boreal forests. These wolves hunt rabbits, birds, deer, and caribou.

Temperate forests

Temperate forests have four seasons—winter, spring, summer, and autumn. Temperate forests receive precipitation all year long. Some temperate forests have **deciduous** trees with broad leaves. The leaves of deciduous trees turn color and drop off the trees in autumn. Temperate **mixed** forests have both conifers and deciduous trees. Temperate **rain forests** receive a lot of rain.

This deer lives in a temperate forest. Which season is it?

Temperate rain forests have tall trees. Many small plants grow on the ground.

Tropical rain forests

Tropical rain forests are close to the equator, where the weather is always sunny and hot. These forests receive a lot of rain each year. Tropical rain forests have tall trees and many other plants. More than half of Earth's plant and animal **species**, or types, can be found in these forests. Tropical rain forests have three levels. They are the **canopy**, or top, the **understory**, or middle, and the **forest floor**, or ground. Different animals live at each level. Monkeys, such as the capuchin shown left, live in the canopy.

This Amazon leaf frog is climbing a vine in the rain forest. It lives in the understory level.

*The emerald tree boa snake lives in rain forests in South America. It eats birds and small **mammals**. It lives in the understory and canopy levels.*

capybara

tapir

Jaguars are big cats that live on the rainforest floor. They hunt deer, capybaras, and tapirs.

13

What are grasslands?

Grasslands are mostly flat lands, where grasses and other small plants grow. Some grasslands also have a few trees. There are two main kinds of grasslands. They are temperate grasslands and **savannas** (see pages 16-17). Temperate grasslands grow in areas with cold winters and warm summers. **Prairies** are temperate grasslands. They can have short or long grasses.

This young mule deer is hiding among some prairie grasses and flowers. Some prairies have very long grasses.

Prairie dogs live in large underground colonies, called **towns**. This prairie dog is eating grass.

This animal is a badger. It also lives under the ground. The badger eats prairie dogs.

This cougar is hunting a badger. Prairie dogs eat grass, badgers eat prairie dogs, and cougars eat badgers. The grass, prairie dog, badger, and cougar form a prairie food chain. The energy of the sun is used by the grass to make food and is passed along to the prairie dog, badger, and cougar.

Huge savannas

Savannas are large grasslands that grow in tropical areas. The temperature is warm year round, and there is a wet season and a dry season. There are different savannas around the world, but the best-known is the Serengeti National Park in East Africa. It is covered with grasses, bushes, and acacia trees. Big animals such as elephants, rhinos, giraffes, and hippos live in this large savanna ecosystem. **Predators** such as lions, cheetahs, and leopards also live there. Predators are animals that hunt and eat other animals.

During the wet season, water covers parts of the savanna.

These cheetah cubs will soon become fierce savanna predators! Cheetahs are very fast runners.

Hippos eat grasses and other plants. They spend most of the day in water and look for food at night, when it is cooler.

Zebras feed on the grasses of the savanna. These zebras have come to drink water at a river.

Hot, dry deserts

A desert is a biome that receives less than 10 inches (25 cm) of rain each year. The plants and animals that live in deserts have adapted to the lack of water. There are different kinds of deserts. Some have more plants and animals than others. The Sahara Desert in Africa is the world's largest hot desert. It is mainly sand, with very few plants or animals living on it.

This camel lives in the Sahara Desert—a hot, dry, sandy desert. There is not much water there. A camel can go up to two weeks without water. Its hump is made of fat. The fat gives the camel's body the energy it needs. Besides drinking, the camel also gets water from the plants it eats.

In some parts of sandy deserts, there is water under the ground. The water comes up in openings. A desert area with water is called an **oasis**. This oasis is in the Sahara Desert. Plants such as palms grow in desert oases. Palms are large plants, but they are not trees.

The long legs of the ostrich keep the ostrich's body above the hot desert sand.

The large ears of the fennec fox allow heat to escape from the fennec's body. The big ears also help the fox hear insects at night. The fox hunts and eats insects.

19

The Sonoran Desert

Some deserts are not too dry or too hot for plants or animals. The Sonoran Desert in southwest United States is a desert habitat where many kinds of plants and animals can be found. Plants called cacti grow there. Cacti have thick, waxy skin and **spines**, or needles.

This coyote finds some shade among these cactus plants. The thick skin of cacti hold in water. Instead of wide leaves, cacti have thin spines. Spines do not allow the water in the plant to **evaporate**, *or turn to vapor, the way wide leaves would.*

Burrowing owls live in underground **burrows**, or holes, where it is cool. They hunt at night.

This lizard is eating a smaller lizard. There is plenty of food to eat in this desert.

Like fennec foxes, jackrabbits have very long ears that help their bodies keep cool.

Two kinds of tundra

Tundra is the coldest biome. There are two kinds of tundra. The **Arctic** tundra is close to the North Pole, and the **alpine** tundra is at the top of very high mountains. The plants in both kinds of tundra grow close to the ground. There are no trees. On mountaintops, trees or tall plants would get blown over by strong winds. On the Arctic tundra, the ground under the soil is always frozen, so the roots of trees cannot grow down into the ground.

This marmot lives high on a mountain. Its home is the alpine tundra.

This caribou lives in the Arctic tundra in summer, where there are many plants to eat. In winter, the caribou must move to forests to find food. The winter tundra is covered with ice and snow.

The Arctic fox has thick fur and a lot of body fat. Its short, thick ears keep body heat inside the fox's body. Furry paws allow the fox to walk on ice and snow in search of food. The Arctic fox can hear animals under the snow. It breaks through the snow to catch and eat them. The fox eats lemmings, mice, ground squirrels, and anything else it can find.

The marine biome

The word "marine" means anything to do with oceans. Oceans are large bodies of salt water. They are very deep in some places. Few plants or animals live in the dark, deep ocean waters. In tropical areas, the ocean is warm and shallow near **seashores**, where oceans meet land. At rocky seashores, water splashes over the rocks and forms **tide pools**. Crabs, sea stars, clams, and sea urchins are trapped in the pools and are eaten by birds and other animals.

a tide pool

sea star   clam   crayfish   limpet   sea urchin

Seaweed called **kelp** grows in oceans. Some kelp grows in huge undersea forests. Kelp are like plants, but they do not have roots. Instead of stems, kelp have **stipes**. Instead of leaves, they have **blades**.

kelp

This squid lives in deep, dark ocean waters.

The water is freezing cold. Very few animals can live in the cold, dark parts of oceans.

Dolphins and whales swim near the **surface**, or top, of oceans, far from shore.

25

Coral reefs

octopus

Coral reefs are ocean habitats with many kinds of fish and other animals. They are found in warm, sunny shallow oceans. Coral reefs are made up of small animals called corals. Besides fish and corals, animals such as sea slugs, sea turtles, and octopuses also live in coral reefs or visit them to find food.

This green sea turtle is visiting a coral reef. Green sea turtles eat sea grasses.

sea slug

sea turtle

corals

Flowing together

An **estuary** is an area where a river flows into an ocean. Estuaries are part of the marine biome. They contain **brackish** water. Brackish water is a mixture of fresh water from a river and salt water from an ocean.

ocean

estuary

Mangroves are trees that grow in estuaries near tropical oceans. They have thick, twisted roots that help keep mud from being carried out to oceans. The mud builds up to form new land.

estuary

river

The freshwater biome

The water in the freshwater biome has very little salt in it.
Streams and rivers, ponds and lakes, and wetlands make
up the freshwater biome. Rivers and streams are bodies of
flowing water that move in one direction. They start on hills
or mountains and flow downward toward oceans, lakes, or
other rivers. The water in both ponds and lakes moves slowly
or is still. Lakes can be huge! Ponds are much smaller. Wetlands
are land areas that are covered with water for most of the year.

These horses are beside a lake. The lake formed from snow that melted on the mountains.

This young hippo lives in a river. It stays in the water all day to keep cool. In the late afternoon, it leaves the river to find food. The birds beside the hippo are also looking for food.

Grasses, reeds, and flowers grow in wetland swamps and marshes. Frogs, alligators, raccoons, and millions of birds live in wetlands or visit them. This great blue heron lives in a wetland swamp. It has found a catfish to eat. Wetlands are very important ecosystems!

Which biome is it?

Guess which kind of biome is shown in each of these pictures. There are clues under the pictures. If you cannot remember the biome names, read pages 8-9 again.

This bird family finds food in this pond. To which biome does the pond belong? Its water is not salty.

These dholes live in a habitat with many trees. Which biome has many trees?

This giraffe lives in a hot, grassy area with acacia trees. What is the biome?

This biome is very dry. Many of the plants that grow here have thick skin and spines.

This biome can be high up on mountains. It has no trees. Plants grow close to the ground.

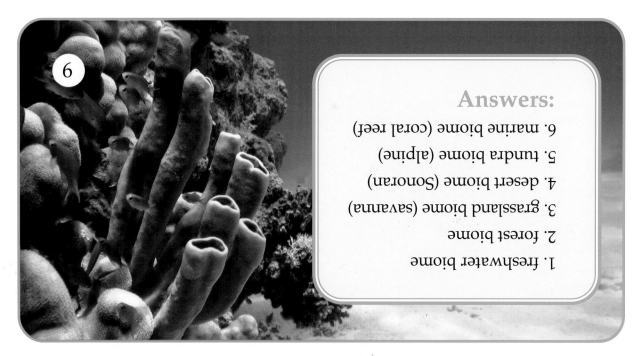

This biome has salt water. Many kinds of fish and other animals live in this biome.

Glossary

Note: Some boldfaced words are defined where they appear in the book.

adapt To become different to suit a new habitat

climate The usual weather that an area has had for a long time

conifer A tree with needles and cones, which stay on a tree all year long

deciduous Describing a tree that sheds its leaves during certain seasons

energy The power living things need to move, eat, grow, and stay alive

equator An imaginary line around the center of Earth, dividing it into north and south

habitat The natural home of an animal

mammal A warm-blooded animal that has hair or fur and drinks milk from its mother's body

precipitation Any form of water, such as rain or snow, which falls to the Earth's surface

predator An animal that hunts and eats other animals

rain forest A forest that receives more than 80 inches (200 cm) of rain a year

species Types of plants or animals that can make new living things together

spine A sharp, needle-like leaf

temperate Describing areas that are between the poles and the equator

tide pool A pool filled with ocean water that forms at a rocky seashore and traps sea creatures

tropical Describing areas near the equator, which have hot climates

wetland An area of land that is under shallow water for part or all of the year

Index

Printed in the U.S.A.—BG